Jackie
Robinson

by Wil Mara

Content Consultant

Nanci R. Vargus, Ed.D.
Professor Emeritus, University of Indianapolis

Reading Consultant

Jeanne Clidas, Ph.D.
Reading Specialist

Children's Press®
An Imprint of Scholastic Inc.
New York Toronto London Auckland Sydney
Mexico City New Delhi Hong Kong
Danbury, Connecticut

Library of Congress Cataloging-in-Publication Data
Mara, Wil.
 Jackie Robinson/by Wil Mara; content consultant, Nanci R. Vargus, Ed.D. professor
emeritus, University of Indianapolis; reading consultant Jeanne Clidas, Ph.D.
     pages cm. — (Rookie biographies)
     Includes index.
     ISBN 978-0-531-21062-8 (library binding) — ISBN 978-0-531-24983-3 (pbk.)
1. Robinson, Jackie, 1919-1972—Juvenile literature. 2. Baseball players—United States—
Biography—Juvenile literature. 3. African American baseball players—Biography—
Juvenile literature. I. Title.
 GV865.R6M37 2014
 796.357092—dc23 [B]   2013034810

Produced by Spooky Cheetah Press
Poem by Jodie Shepherd
Design by Keith Plechaty

© 2014 by Scholastic Inc.

Printed in China 62

SCHOLASTIC, CHILDREN'S PRESS, ROOKIE BIOGRAPHIES®, and associated logos
are trademarks and/or registered trademarks of Scholastic Inc.

9 10 R 23 22 21 20 19

Photographs © 2014: AP Images: 4, 30 left; Corbis Images/Bettmann: 23 (Frank
Jurkoski), 19, 27; Everett Collection: 11; Getty Images: 12 (Archive Photos), 8, 31 bottom
(Hulton Archive), 3 top, 31 top (Kevin Winter), cover, 30 right (MLB Photos/Hulton
Archive), 15 (Murray Garrett/Hulton Archive), 24 (National Baseball Hall of Fame
Library/MLB Photos); iStockphoto/devonanne: 31 center top; Library of Congress/
John Vachon: 31 center bottom; Negro Leagues Baseball Museum: 16; Newscom/
Dustin Snipes/Icon Sports Media: 28; The Granger Collection: 20; Thinkstock/
iStockphoto: 3 bottom.

Maps by XNR Productions, Inc.

Scholastic Inc., 557 Broadway, New York, NY 10012.

Table of Contents

Meet Jackie Robinson 5

Changing History 18

One of the Best Ever 22

Timeline. 28

A Poem About Jackie Robinson 30

You Can Be Courageous 30

Glossary 31

Index. 32

Facts for Now 32

About the Author 32

Meet Jackie Robinson

Jackie Robinson was one of the greatest baseball players of all time. He was the first African American to ever play on a team of all white players. He inspired millions and changed the game of baseball forever.

When Jackie played for the Dodgers, he wore number 42.

Jackie Roosevelt Robinson was born in Cairo, Georgia, on January 31, 1919. He had three brothers and one sister. Jackie's father left the family the year after Jackie was born. His mother moved the family to California and raised the children on her own.

Jackie was born in Cairo, Georgia.

Tennessee

MAP KEY

Georgia

● Town where Jackie Robinson was born

South Carolina

Georgia

Alabama

Cairo

ATLANTIC OCEAN

Florida

Gulf of Mexico

This is a photo of Jackie *(second from left)* with his mother and his siblings.

At the time, African Americans were treated badly in many places in the United States. Some white people did not want a black family living in their neighborhood. Jackie and his **siblings** were called names. Once a neighbor even threw rocks at Jackie. But his mom would not move.

Jackie was a great athlete. In high school he won several **awards**. At junior college, Jackie was the starting quarterback on the football team. He was voted Most Valuable Player (MVP) on an all-star baseball team and broke records in track and field.

FAST FACT!

Jackie's brother Mack was also an excellent athlete. He won one gold and one silver medal in track and field at the 1936 Olympic Games in Berlin, Germany.

This is a photo of Jackie playing football.

Jackie and Rachel
got married in 1946.

Jackie moved to the University of California at Los Angeles (UCLA) in 1939. He played four different sports—basketball, football, baseball, and track. During his senior year, Jackie was named the best all-around athlete on the West Coast.

While at college, Jackie met Rachel Isum. They later married and had three children together.

Jackie became a soldier during World War II. Once again, he faced poor treatment because he was black. He left the army after two years.

In 1945, Jackie began playing baseball for a team called the Kansas City Monarchs. The team was part of the Negro League.

At this time, a lot of America was **segregated**. Major League Baseball (MLB) had only white players. In some places, African Americans could not eat in the same restaurants as whites. African American children could not go to the same schools as white children.

Here, Jackie *(right)* poses with teammate Satchel Paige, another Negro League superstar.

Changing History

Branch Rickey wanted to end segregation in baseball. He needed a super athlete. He also wanted a strong person who would not get upset when angry people called him names. Branch chose Jackie to play for his team, the Brooklyn Dodgers.

This photo was taken when Jackie signed his contract with Branch Rickey.

This photo shows Jackie stealing home.

Jackie started playing for the Dodgers on April 15, 1947. People called him terrible names. Some even threatened to kill him! Other players tried to hurt him, too. They hit him with pitches and kicked him with their **cleats**. Jackie fought back by becoming one of the best players in the game.

FAST FACT!

The Dodgers started out in Brooklyn, New York. They moved to Los Angeles, California, in 1957.

One of the Best Ever

Jackie's hard work paid off. In 1947, he was named baseball's Rookie of the Year. In 1949, he was the league MVP. Fans and players began to change their minds about him—and about black players in general. Soon, talented black players were joining MLB teams.

Negro League players Roy Campanella *(left)* and Don Newcombe *(center)* joined Jackie on the Dodgers.

Jackie's wife and mother were with him when he went into the National Baseball Hall of Fame.

Jackie retired from baseball after the 1956 season. He showed that a black player could be every bit as good as a white one. Even more important, he opened Major League Baseball to nonwhite players.

FAST FACT!

In 1962, Jackie became the first black player to be voted into baseball's Hall of Fame.

After baseball Jackie continued to work to make life better for African Americans. Sadly, Jackie died of a heart attack when he was only 53 years old.

Jackie is shown here with Martin Luther King Jr. and other civil rights leaders.

Timeline of Jackie Robinson's Life

1919
born on January 31

1939
becomes a star athlete at UCLA

1945
begins playing for the Kansas City Monarchs

In 1977, Major League Baseball retired Jackie's number, 42. No other player will ever be allowed to wear it again—except on April 15th, Jackie Robinson Day. Then, every player wears number 42 to honor one of the most important people in sports history.

1946
marries Rachel Isum

1955
helps Dodgers win World Series

1947
begins playing for the Brooklyn Dodgers

1972
dies on October 24

29

A Poem About Jackie Robinson

Hip hip hooray for 42—
a baseball star, and a brave man, too.
He ignored the nay-sayers and put them to shame
and so forever changed the game.

You Can Be Courageous

- Work hard at something if you believe it is right, even if others try to stop you.

- Always try to be the best at whatever you do.

- Be willing to fight for change if you believe that change is for the better.

- Stand up for what you believe. Help others who need support.

Glossary

awards (uh-WORDS): prizes

cleats (CLEETS): shoes that have spikes on the bottom

segregated (seg-ree-GAY-ted): when people and/or groups are kept apart

siblings (SIB-lings): brothers or sisters

Index

army 14

baseball 5, 10, 13, 14, 17, 18, 22, 25, 26, 29

Brooklyn Dodgers 18, 21

college 10, 13

death 26

early life 6–13

family 13

Kansas City Monarchs 14

Major League Baseball (MLB) 17, 22, 29

Most Valuable Player 10, 22

National Baseball Hall of Fame 25

Negro League 14

Rickey, Branch 18

segregation 17, 18

Facts for Now

Visit this Scholastic Web site for more information on Jackie Robinson:
www.factsfornow.scholastic.com
Enter the keywords **Jackie Robinson**

About the Author

Wil Mara is the award-winning author of more than one hundred and 140 books. Many are educational titles for children.